MW00681607

To

From

Date

Promises from God for Mother

Designed by Christian Art Gifts

Compiled by Annegreth Botha

Printed in China

ISBN 978-1-86920-758-8

07 08 09 10 11 12 13 14 15 16 – 10 9 8 7 6 5 4 3 2 1

Promises from God for *Mother*

christian art gifts®

Contents

Appearance

Know that the LORD is God. It is he who made us, and we are his; we are his people, the sheep of his pasture.

Psalm 100:3

For we are His workmanship, created in Christ Jesus for good works, which God prepared beforehand that we should walk in them.

Ephesians 2:10 NKJV

"Do not be afraid, for I have ransomed you. I have called you by name; you are mine."

Isaiah 43:1 NLT

For the LORD takes delight in his people; he crowns the humble with salvation.

Psalm 149:4

You know me inside and out, you know every bone in my body; you know exactly how I was made, bit by bit, how I was sculpted from nothing into something.

Psalm 139:15 The Message

The Lord said to Samuel, "Do not look on his appearance or on the height of his stature. For the Lord sees not as man sees: man looks on the outward appearance, but the Lord looks on the heart."

1 Samuel 16:7 ESV

I praise you because I am fearfully and wonderfully made; your works are wonderful, I know that full well.

Psalm 139:14

You judge by appearances. If any of you think you are the only ones who belong to Christ, then think again. We belong to Christ as much as you do.

2 Corinthians 10:7 CEV

The LORD has appeared to me, saying: "Yes, I have loved you with an everlasting love; therefore with lovingkindness I have drawn you."

Jeremiah 31:3 NKJV

Your beauty should not come from outward adornment. Instead, it should be that of your inner self, the unfading beauty of a gentle and quiet spirit.

1 Peter 3:3-4

Charm is deceptive, and beauty is fleeting; but a woman who fears the LORD is to be praised.

Proverbs 31:30

Reflections on Appearance

Blessings

Oh, the joys of those who do not follow the advice of the wicked, or stand around with sinners, of join in with scoffers. But they delight in doing everything the LORD wants; day and night they think about his law.

Psalm 1:1-2 NLT

But He gives more grace. Therefore He says: "God resists the proud, but gives grace to the humble."

James 4:6 NKJV

Bless the LORD, O my soul, and forget not all his benefits, who forgives all your iniquity, who heals all your diseases.

Psalm 103:2-3 ESV

The blessing of the LORD makes one rich, and He adds no sorrow with it.

Proverbs 10:22 NKJV

Open your mouth and taste, open your eyes and see – how good GOD is. Blessed are you who run to him.

Psalm 34:8 THE MESSAGE

"Blessed are those who trust in the LORD and have made the LORD their hope and confidence."

Jeremiah 17:7 NLT

The LORD bless you and keep you; the LORD make his face to shine upon you and be gracious to you; the LORD lift up his countenance upon you and give you peace.

Numbers 6:24-26 ESV

See, I am setting before you today a blessing and a curse – the blessing if you obey the commands of the LORD your God that I am giving you today.

Deuteronomy 11:26-27

Don't repay evil for evil. Don't retaliate when people say unkind things about you. Instead, pay them back with a blessing. That is what God wants you to do, and he will bless you for it.

1 Peter 3:9 NLT

Blessed is he who has regard for the weak;
the LORD delivers him in times of trouble.

Psalm 41:1

"Blessed is she who believed that there would be a fulfillment of what was spoken to her from the Lord."

Luke 1:45 ESV

The LORD will give strength to His people;
the LORD will bless His people with peace.

Psalm 29:11 NKJV

Reflections on Blessings

Children

Grandchildren are the crowning glory of the aged; parents are the pride of their children.

Proverbs 17:6 NLT

Train a child in the way he should go, and when he is old he will not turn from it.

Proverbs 22:6

"Believe on the Lord Jesus Christ, and you will be saved, you and your household."

Acts 16:31 NKJV

All your children shall be taught by the LORD, and great shall be the peace of your children.

Isaiah 54:13 ESV

From the lips of children and infants you have ordained praise.

Psalm 8:2

"I will give them one heart and mind to worship me forever, for their own good and for the good of all their descendants."

Jeremiah 32:39 NLT

I have no greater joy than to hear that my children are walking in the truth.

3 John 4 ESV

Even a child is known by his actions, by whether his conduct is pure and right.

Proverbs 20:11

He took a little child and set him in the midst of them. And when He had taken him in His arms, He said to them, "Whoever receives one of these little children in My name receives Me; and whoever receives Me, receives not Me but Him who sent Me."

Mark 9:36-37 NKJV

Behold, children are a heritage from the LORD, the fruit of the womb a reward. Like arrows in the hand of a warrior are the children of one's youth.

Psalm 127:3-4 ESV

From everlasting to everlasting the LORD's love is with those who fear him, and his righteousness with their children's children.

Psalm 103:17

Happy are those who fear the LORD. Yes, happy are those who delight in doing what he commands. Their children will be successful everywhere; an entire generation of godly people will be blessed.

Psalm 112:1-2 NLT

Reflections on Children

Comfort

"As a mother comforts her child, so will I comfort you."

Isaiah 66:13

The Lord will lead you into the land. He will always be with you and help you, so don't ever be afraid of your enemies.

Deuteronomy 31:8 CEV

Cast your burden on the Lord, and He shall sustain you; He shall never permit the righteous to be moved.

Psalm 55:22 NKJV

The Lord is good, a stronghold in the day of trouble; he knows those who take refuge in him.

Nahum 1:7 ESV

"I am leaving you with a gift – peace of mind and heart. And the peace I give isn't like the peace the world gives. So don't be troubled or afraid."

John 14:27 NLT

Cast all your anxiety on him because he cares for you.

1 Peter 5:7

"Come to Me, all you who labor and are heavy laden, and I will give you rest."

Matthew 11:28 NKJV

You will restore me to even greater honor and comfort me once again.

Psalm 71:21 NLT

Comfort, comfort my people, says your God.

Isaiah 40:1

Share each other's troubles and problems, and in this way obey the law of Christ.

Galatians 6:2 NLT

All praise to the God and Father of our Master, Jesus the Messiah! Father of all mercy! God of all healing counsel! He comes alongside us when we go through hard times, and before you know it, he brings us alongside someone else who is going through hard times so that we can be there for that person just as God was there for us.

2 Corinthians 1:3-4 The Message

"I will not leave you as orphans; I will come to you."

John 14:18 ESV

Reflections on Comfort

Compassion

Your compassion is great, O LORD; preserve my life according to your laws.

Psalm 119:156

"You are a God of forgiveness, gracious and merciful, slow to become angry, and full of unfailing love and mercy."

Nehemiah 9:17 NLT

Through the LORD's mercies we are not consumed, because His compassions fail not. They are new every morning; great is Your faithfulness.

Lamentations 3:22-23 NKJV

The LORD is good to all, and his mercy is over all that he has made.

Psalm 145:9 ESV

Therefore, as God's chosen people, holy and dearly loved, clothe yourselves with compassion, kindness, humility, gentleness and patience. Bear with each other and forgive whatever grievances you may have against one another. Forgive as the Lord forgave you.

Colossians 3:12-13

The LORD your God is gracious and merciful and will not turn away his face from you, if you return to him.

2 Chronicles 30:9 ESV

He has made His wonderful works to be remembered; the LORD is gracious and full of compassion.

Psalm 111:4 NKJV

The LORD is like a father to his children, tender and compassionate to those who fear him.

Psalm 103:13 NLT

The Lord is full of compassion and mercy.

James 5:11

All of you be of one mind, having compassion for one another; love as brothers, be tenderhearted, be courteous, knowing that you were called to this, that you may inherit a blessing.

1 Peter 3:8-9 NKJV

You will again have compassion on us; you will tread our sins underfoot and hurl all our iniquities into the depths of the sea.

Micah 7:19

You, O Lord, are a God merciful and gracious, slow to anger and abounding in steadfast love and faithfulness.

Psalm 86:15 ESV

Reflections on Compassion

Courage

Be strong and courageous. Do not be terrified; do not be discouraged, for the LORD your God will be with you wherever you go.

Joshua 1:9

In the day when I cried out, You answered me, and made me bold with strength in my soul.

Psalm 138:3 NKJV

For I can do everything with the help of Christ who gives me the strength I need.

Philippians 4:13 NLT

Because the Sovereign LORD helps me, I will not be disgraced.

Isaiah 50:7

"Fear not, for I am with you; be not dismayed, for I am your God; I will strengthen you, I will help you, I will uphold you with my righteous right hand."

Isaiah 41:10 ESV

Christ is faithful as a son over God's house. And we are his house, if we hold on to our courage and the hope of which we boast.

Hebrews 3:6

You protect me with salvation-armor; you hold me up with a firm hand, caress me with your gentle ways. You cleared the ground under me so my footing was firm.

Psalm 18:32-33 The Message

"Be strong and courageous, for your work will be rewarded."

2 Chronicles 15:7 NLT

Be of good courage, and He shall strengthen your heart, all you who hope in the LORD.

Psalm 31:24 NKJV

He gives power to the faint, and to him who has no might he increases strength.

Isaiah 40:29 ESV

So do not throw away your confidence; it will be richly rewarded. You need to persevere so that when you have done the will of God, you will receive what he has promised.

Hebrews 10:35-36

The wicked are edgy with guilt, ready to run off even when no one's after them; honest people are relaxed and confident, bold as lions.

Proverbs 28:1 THE MESSAGE

Reflections on Courage

Faith

"Have faith in God," Jesus answered. "I tell you the truth, if anyone says to this mountain, 'Go, throw yourself into the sea,' and does not doubt in his heart but believes that what he says will happen, it will be done for him."

Mark 11:22-23

"Believe in the LORD your God, and you will be able to stand firm."

2 Chronicles 20:20 NLT

"Truly, truly, I say to you, whoever believes has eternal life."

John 6:47 ESV

The prayer of faith will save the sick, and the Lord will raise him up. And if he has committed sins, he will be forgiven.

James 5:15 NKJV

Know that the LORD your God, He is God, the faithful God who keeps covenant and mercy for a thousand generations with those who love Him and keep His commandments.

Deuteronomy 7:9 NKJV

The LORD rewards every man for his righteousness and faithfulness.

1 Samuel 26:23

God has dealt to each one a measure of faith.

Romans 12:3 NKJV

Every child of God can defeat the world, and our faith is what gives us this victory.

1 John 5:4 CEV

By entering through faith into what God has always wanted to do for us – set us right with him, make us fit for him – we have it all together with God because of our Master Jesus.

Romans 5:1 The Message

So, you see, it is impossible to please God without faith. Anyone who wants to come to him must believe that there is a God and that he rewards those who sincerely seek him.

Hebrews 11:6 NLT

"Believe in the Lord Jesus, and you will be saved – you and your household."

Acts 16:31

Though you have not seen him, you love him. Though you do not now see him, you believe in him and rejoice with joy that is inexpressible and filled with glory, obtaining the outcome of your faith, the salvation of your souls.

1 Peter 1:8-9 ESV

Reflections on Faith

Family

So now Jesus and the ones he makes holy have the same Father. That is why Jesus is not ashamed to call them his brothers and sisters.

Hebrews 2:11 NLT

My father and my mother have forsaken me, but the LORD will take me in.

Psalm 27:10 ESV

How great is the love the Father has lavished on us, that we should be called children of God! And that is what we are!

1 John 3:1

"Whoever does the will of God, he is my brother and sister and mother."

Mark 3:35 ESV

For this reason I bow my knees to the Father of our Lord Jesus Christ, from whom the whole family in heaven and earth is named.

Ephesians 3:14-15 NKJV

Good friend, follow your father's good advice; don't wander off from your mother's teachings. Wrap yourself in them from head to foot; wear them like a scarf around your neck. Wherever you walk, they'll guide you; whenever you rest, they'll guard you; when you wake up, they'll tell you what's next.

Proverbs 6:20-22 The Message

As a father has compassion on his children, so the Lord has compassion on those who fear him.

Psalm 103:13

"Honor your father and mother. Then you will live a long, full life in the land the Lord your God will give you."

Exodus 20:12 NLT

Train up a child in the way he should go, and when he is old he will not depart from it.

Proverbs 22:6 NKJV

When I left the womb you cradled me; since the moment of birth you've been my God.

Psalm 22:10 The Message

Father to the fatherless, defender of widows – this is God, whose dwelling is holy. God places the lonely in families; he sets the prisoners free and gives them joy.

Psalm 68:5-6 NLT

"I will be a Father to you, and you will be my sons and daughters, says the Lord."

2 Corinthians 6:18

Reflections on Family

Forgiveness

If My people who are called by My name will humble themselves, and pray and seek My face, and turn from their wicked ways, then I will hear from heaven, and will forgive their sin and heal their land.

2 Chronicles 7:14 NKJV

If we confess our sins, he is faithful and just to forgive us our sins and to cleanse us from all unrighteousness.

1 John 1:9 ESV

"When you stand praying, if you hold anything against anyone, forgive him, so that your Father in heaven may forgive you your sins."

Mark 11:25

Don't ever say, "I'll get you for that!" Wait for GOD; he'll settle the score.

Proverbs 20:22 THE MESSAGE

You must make allowance for each other's faults and forgive the person who offends you. Remember, the Lord forgave you, so you must forgive others.

Colossians 3:13 NLT

You forgave the iniquity of your people; you covered all their sin.

Psalm 85:2 ESV

"I, even I, am he who blots out your transgressions, for my own sake, and remembers your sins no more."

Isaiah 43:25

"I will forgive their wrongdoings, and I will never again remember their sins," says the Lord.

Hebrews 8:12 NLT

"Give, and it will be given to you. A good measure, pressed down, shaken together and running over, will be poured into your lap. For with the measure you use, it will be measured to you."

Luke 6:38

In him we have redemption through his blood, the forgiveness of our trespasses, according to the riches of his grace.

Ephesians 1:7 ESV

"For if you forgive men their trespasses, your heavenly Father will also forgive you. But if you do not forgive men their trespasses, neither will your Father forgive your trespasses."

Matthew 6:14-15 NKJV

"Come now, let us reason together," says the LORD. "Though your sins are like scarlet, they shall be as white as snow; though they are red as crimson, they shall be like wool."

Isaiah 1:18

Reflections on Forgiveness

Friendship

We know what real love is because Christ gave up his life for us. And so we also ought to give up our lives for our Christian brothers and sisters.

1 John 3:16 NLT

A friend loves at all times, and a brother is born for adversity.

Proverbs 17:17 NKJV

"For where two or three come together in my name, there am I with them."

Matthew 18:20

"Greater love has no one than this, that someone lays down his life for his friends."

John 15:13 ESV

Jonathan said to David, "Go in peace, because we have sworn both of us in the name of the LORD, saying, 'The LORD shall be between me and you, and between my offspring and your offspring, forever.'"

1 Samuel 20:42 ESV

Share each other's troubles and problems, and in this way obey the law of Christ.

Galatians 6:2 NLT

"You are My friends if you do whatever I command you. No longer do I call you servants, for a servant does not know what his master is doing; but I have called you friends."

John 15:14-15 NKJV

Perfume and incense bring joy to the heart, and the pleasantness of one's friend springs from his earnest counsel.

Proverbs 27:9

My intercessor is my friend as my eyes pour out tears to God; on behalf of a man he pleads with God as a man pleads for his friend.

Job 16:20-21

Wounds from a friend are better than many kisses from an enemy.

Proverbs 27:6 NLT

Two are better than one, because they have a good reward for their labor. For if they fall, one will lift up his companion. Though one may be overpowered by another, two can withstand him. And a threefold cord is not quickly broken.

Ecclesiastes 4:9-10, 12 NKJV

Anyone who loves a pure heart and gracious speech is the king's friend.

Proverbs 22:11 NLT

Reflections on Friendship

God's Will

Trust in the LORD with all your heart and lean not on your own understanding; in all your ways acknowledge him, and he will make your paths straight.

Proverbs 3:5-6

Do not be conformed to this world, but be transformed by the renewing of your mind, that you may prove what is that good and acceptable and perfect will of God.

Romans 12:2 NKJV

He has showed you, O man, what is good. And what does the LORD require of you? To act justly and to love mercy and to walk humbly with your God.

Micah 6:8

The steps of the godly are directed by the LORD. He delights in every detail of their lives.

Psalm 37:23 NLT

Jesus said to the people who believed in him, "You are truly my disciples if you keep obeying my teachings. And you will know the truth, and the truth will set you free."

John 8:31-32 NLT

It is God who works in you both to will and to do for His good pleasure.

Philippians 2:13 NKJV

"If anyone's will is to do God's will, he will know whether the teaching is from God or whether I am speaking on my own authority."

John 7:17 ESV

Give thanks in all circumstances; for this is the will of God in Christ Jesus for you.

1 Thessalonians 5:18 ESV

If you call out for insight and cry aloud for understanding, and if you look for it as for silver and search for it as for hidden treasure, then you will understand the fear of the LORD and find the knowledge of God.

Proverbs 2:3-5

"Here are My mother and My brothers! For whoever does the will of God is My brother, and My sister and mother."

Mark 3:34-35 NKJV

So if you are suffering according to God's will, keep on doing what is right, and trust yourself to the God who made you, for he will never fail you.

1 Peter 4:19 NLT

You need to persevere so that when you have done the will of God, you will receive what he has promised.

Hebrews 10:36

Reflections on God's Will

Gossip

The mouth of the righteous man utters wisdom, and his tongue speaks what is just. The law of his God is in his heart; his feet do not slip.

Psalm 37:30-31

He who goes about as a talebearer reveals secrets; therefore do not associate with one who flatters with his lips.

Proverbs 20:19 NKJV

A gadabout gossip can't be trusted with a secret, but someone of integrity won't violate a confidence.

Proverbs 11:13 The Message

What dainty morsels rumors are – but they sink deep into one's heart.

Proverbs 18:8 NLT

Though some tongues just love the taste of gossip, Christians have better uses for language than that. Don't talk dirty or silly. That kind of talk doesn't fit our style. Thanksgiving is our dialect.

Ephesians 5:4 THE MESSAGE

I refuse to shake hands with those who plan evil. I put a gag on the gossip who bad-mouths his neighbor.

Psalm 101:4-5 THE MESSAGE

Who may worship in your sanctuary, LORD? Who may enter your presence on your holy hill? Those who lead blameless lives and do what is right, speaking the truth from sincere hearts. Those who refuse to slander others or harm their neighbors or speak evil of their friends. Such people will stand firm forever.

Psalm 15:1-3, 5 NLT

"Do not go about spreading slander among your people. Do not do anything that endangers your neighbor's life. I am the LORD."

Leviticus 19:16

Listening to gossip is like eating cheap candy; do you want junk like that in your belly?

Proverbs 26:22 THE MESSAGE

Without wood a fire goes out; without gossip a quarrel dies down. As charcoal to embers and as wood to fire, so is a quarrelsome man for kindling strife.

Proverbs 26:20-21

Let the lying lips be put to silence, which speak insolent things proudly and contemptuously against the righteous.

Psalm 31:18 NKJV

Reflections on Gossip

Happiness

You have made known to me the path of life; you will fill me with joy in your presence, with eternal pleasures at your right hand.

Psalm 16:11

Behold, happy is the man whom God corrects; therefore do not despise the chastening of the Almighty.

Job 5:17 NKJV

I know the LORD is always with me. I will not be shaken, for he is right beside me. No wonder my heart is filled with joy, and my mouth shouts his praises!

Psalm 16:8-9 NLT

"His master replied, 'Well done, good and faithful servant! You have been faithful with a few things; I will put you in charge of many things. Come and share your master's happiness!'"

Matthew 25:23

God gives wisdom, knowledge, and joy to those who please him.

Ecclesiastes 2:26 NLT

Happy are those who fear the LORD. Yes, happy are those who delight in doing what he commands.

Psalm 112:1 NLT

Blessed is every one who fears the LORD, who walks in His ways. When you eat the labor of your hands, you shall be happy, and it shall be well with you.

Psalm 128:1-2 NKJV

A happy heart makes the face cheerful, but heartache crushes the spirit.

Proverbs 15:13

Is any one of you in trouble? He should pray. Is anyone happy? Let him sing songs of praise. Is any one of you sick? He should call the elders of the church to pray over him and anoint him with oil in the name of the Lord. And the prayer offered in faith will make the sick person well; the Lord will raise him up. If he has sinned, he will be forgiven.

James 5:13-15

Happy are the people who are in such a state; happy are the people whose God is the LORD!

Psalm 144:15 NKJV

Happy is the person who finds wisdom and gains understanding. For the profit of wisdom is better than silver, and her wages are better than gold.

Proverbs 3:13-14 NLT

Happy are those who have the God of Israel as their helper, whose hope is in the LORD their God.

Psalm 146:5 NLT

Reflections on Happiness

Honesty

Don't lie to each other, for you have stripped off your old evil nature and all its wicked deeds. In its place you have clothed yourselves with a brand-new nature that is continually being renewed as you learn more and more about Christ, who created this new nature within you.

Colossians 3:9-10 NLT

The LORD abhors dishonest scales, but accurate weights are his delight.

Proverbs 11:1

If you weigh and measure things honestly, the LORD your God will let you enjoy a long life in the land he is giving you.

Deuteronomy 25:15 CEV

Whatever is true, whatever is noble, whatever is right, whatever is pure, whatever is lovely, whatever is admirable – if anything is excellent or praiseworthy – think about such things. And the God of peace will be with you.

Philippians 4:8-9

Honesty lives confident and carefree, but Shifty is sure to be exposed.

Proverbs 10:9 The Message

Better is a little with righteousness, than vast revenues without justice.

Proverbs 16:8 NKJV

I know, my God, that you test the heart and are pleased with integrity. All these things have I given willingly and with honest intent.

1 Chronicles 29:17

He who speaks truth declares righteousness, but a false witness, deceit.

Proverbs 12:17 NKJV

"As for that in the good soil, they are those who, hearing the word, hold it fast in an honest and good heart, and bear fruit with patience."

Luke 8:15 ESV

It is an honor to receive an honest reply.

Proverbs 24:26 NLT

Kings take pleasure in honest lips; they value a man who speaks the truth.

Proverbs 16:13

Reflections on Honesty

Honor

You made us only a little lower than God, and you crowned us with glory and honor.

Psalm 8:5 NLT

"Whoever serves me must follow me; and where I am, my servant also will be. My Father will honor the one who serves me."

John 12:26

Honor the LORD with your wealth and with the firstfruits of all your produce; then your barns will be filled with plenty, and your vats will be bursting with wine.

Proverbs 3:9-10 ESV

"Honor your father and mother. Then you will live a long, full life in the land the LORD your God will give you."

Exodus 20:12 NLT

Those members of the body which we think to be less honorable, on these we bestow greater honor. God composed the body, having given greater honor to that part which lacks it.

1 Corinthians 12:23-24 NKJV

He will call upon me, and I will answer him; I will be with him in trouble, I will deliver him and honor him.

Psalm 91:15

All may honor the Son, just as they honor the Father. Whoever does not honor the Son does not honor the Father who sent him.

John 5:23 ESV

Give honor to marriage, and remain faithful to one another in marriage. God will surely judge people who are immoral.

Hebrews 13:4 NLT

Daughters of kings are among your honored women. The king is enthralled by your beauty; honor him, for he is your lord.

Psalm 45:9, 11

Children, obey your parents in the Lord, for this is right. "Honor your father and mother," which is the first commandment with promise: "that it may be well with you and you may live long on the earth."

Ephesians 6:1-3 NKJV

Reflections on Honor

Hope

Blessed be the God and Father of our Lord Jesus Christ, who according to His abundant mercy has begotten us again to a living hope through the resurrection of Jesus Christ from the dead.

1 Peter 1:3 NKJV

Our hope is in the living God, who is the Savior of all people, and particularly of those who believe.

1 Timothy 4:10 NLT

He delivered us from such a deadly peril, and he will deliver us. On him we have set our hope that he will deliver us again.

2 Corinthians 1:10 ESV

The LORD is good to those whose hope is in him, to the one who seeks him.

Lamentations 3:25

For everything that was written in the past was written to teach us, so that through endurance and the encouragement of the Scriptures we might have hope.

Romans 15:4

There are three things that will endure – faith, hope, and love.

1 Corinthians 13:13 NLT

Let us hold fast the confession of our hope without wavering, for He who promised is faithful.

Hebrews 10:23 NKJV

Blessed is the man who trusts in the LORD, and whose hope is the LORD.

Jeremiah 17:7 NKJV

So be strong and take courage, all you who put your hope in the LORD!

Psalm 31:24 NLT

I pray also that the eyes of your heart may be enlightened in order that you may know the hope to which he has called you, the riches of his glorious inheritance in the saints, and his incomparably great power for us who believe.

Ephesians 1:18-19

May the God of hope fill you with all joy and peace in believing, so that by the power of the Holy Spirit you may abound in hope.

Romans 15:13 ESV

You are my refuge and my shield; I have put my hope in your word.

Psalm 119:114

Reflections on Hope

Integrity

May integrity and honesty protect me, for I put my hope in you.

Psalm 25:21 NLT

Jesus said, "By standing firm you will gain life."

Luke 21:19

As for me, You uphold me in my integrity, and set me before Your face forever.

Psalm 41:12 NKJV

People with integrity have firm footing, but those who follow crooked paths will slip and fall.

Proverbs 10:9 NLT

Light dawns in the darkness for the upright; he is gracious, merciful, and righteous.

Psalm 112:4 ESV

He keeps his eye on all who live honestly, and pays special attention to his loyally committed ones.

Proverbs 2:8 THE MESSAGE

The LORD God is a sun and shield; the LORD will give grace and glory; no good thing will He withhold from those who walk uprightly.

Psalm 84:11 NKJV

Light is shed upon the righteous and joy on the upright in heart.

Psalm 97:11

Good people are guided by their honesty; treacherous people are destroyed by their dishonesty.

Proverbs 11:3 NLT

May God himself, the God of peace, sanctify you through and through. May your whole spirit, soul and body be kept blameless at the coming of our Lord Jesus Christ. The one who calls you is faithful and he will do it.

1 Thessalonians 5:23-24

For only the upright will live in the land, and those who have integrity will remain in it.

Proverbs 2:21 NLT

For the LORD is righteous; he loves righteous deeds; the upright shall behold his face.

Psalm 11:7 ESV

Reflections on Integrity

Joy

Go and enjoy choice food and sweet drinks, and send some to those who have nothing prepared. This day is sacred to our Lord. Do not grieve, for the joy of the LORD is your strength.

Nehemiah 8:10

"I have told you this, so that you might have peace in your hearts because of me. While you are in the world, you will have to suffer. But cheer up! I have defeated the world."

John 16:33 CEV

"So also you have sorrow now, but I will see you again and your hearts will rejoice, and no one will take your joy from you."

John 16:22 ESV

Those who sow in tears shall reap in joy.

Psalm 126:5 NKJV

You have made known to me the path of life; you will fill me with joy in your presence, with eternal pleasures at your right hand.

Psalm 16:11

You have put more joy in my heart than they have when their grain and wine abound.

Psalm 4:7 ESV

You love him even though you have never seen him. Though you do not see him, you trust him; and even now you are happy with a glorious, inexpressible joy. Your reward for trusting him will be the salvation of your souls.

1 Peter 1:8-9 NLT

For our heart is glad in him, because we trust in his holy name.

Psalm 33:21 ESV

The LORD your God will bless you in all your harvest and in all the work of your hands, and your joy will be complete.

Deuteronomy 16:15

"If you keep My commandments, you will abide in My love, just as I have kept My Father's commandments and abide in His love. These things I have spoken to you, that My joy may remain in you, and that your joy may be full."

John 15:10-11 NKJV

He never left himself without a witness. There were always his reminders, such as sending you rain and good crops and giving you food and joyful hearts.

Acts 14:17 NLT

Now may the God of hope fill you with all joy and peace in believing, that you may abound in hope by the power of the Holy Spirit.

Romans 15:13 NKJV

Reflections on Joy

Kindness

"Love your enemies, and do good, and lend, expecting nothing in return, and your reward will be great, and you will be sons of the Most High, for he is kind to the ungrateful and the evil."

Luke 6:35 ESV

Tell the LORD how thankful you are, because he is kind and always merciful.

Psalm 118:1 CEV

When the kindness and love of God our Savior appeared, he saved us, not because of righteous things we had done, but because of his mercy. He saved us through the washing of rebirth and renewal by the Holy Spirit.

Titus 3:4-5

What is desired in a man is kindness, and a poor man is better than a liar. The fear of the LORD leads to life, and he who has it will abide in satisfaction; he will not be visited with evil.

Proverbs 19:22-23 NKJV

"In a surge of anger I hid my face from you for a moment, but with everlasting kindness I will have compassion on you," says the LORD your Redeemer.

Isaiah 54:8

Since God chose you to be the holy people whom he loves, you must clothe yourselves with tenderhearted mercy, kindness, humility, gentleness, and patience. Remember, the Lord forgave you, so you must forgive others.

Colossians 3:12-13 NLT

May you be blessed by the LORD, my daughter. You have made this last kindness greater than the first. And now, my daughter, do not fear.

Ruth 3:10-11 ESV

Who can find a virtuous wife? For her worth is far above rubies. She opens her mouth with wisdom, and on her tongue is the law of kindness. Charm is deceitful and beauty is passing, but a woman who fears the LORD, she shall be praised.

Proverbs 31:10, 26, 30 NKJV

As servants of God we commend ourselves in every way: in purity, understanding, patience and kindness; in the Holy Spirit and in sincere love; poor, yet making many rich; having nothing, and yet possessing everything.

2 Corinthians 6:4, 6, 10

Notice how God is both kind and severe. He is severe to those who disobeyed, but kind to you as you continue to trust in his kindness.

Romans 11:22 NLT

Reflections on Kindness

Love

For I am persuaded that neither death nor life, nor angels nor principalities nor powers, nor things present nor things to come, nor height nor depth, nor any other created thing, shall be able to separate us from the love of God which is in Christ Jesus our Lord.

Romans 8:38-39 NKJV

A friend loves at all times, and a brother is born for adversity.

Proverbs 17:17 ESV

Everyone who believes that Jesus is the Christ is a child of God. And everyone who loves the Father loves his children, too. We know we love God's children if we love God and obey his commandments.

1 John 5:1-2 NLT

As we live in God, our love grows more perfect. So we will not be afraid on the day of judgment, but we can face him with confidence because we are like Christ here in this world. Such love has no fear because perfect love expels all fear. If we are afraid, it is for fear of judgment, and this shows that his love has not been perfected in us.

1 John 4:17-18 NLT

Love each other deeply, because love covers over a multitude of sins.

1 Peter 4:8

"For God so loved the world that he gave his one and only Son, that whoever believes in him shall not perish but have eternal life."

John 3:16

The LORD appeared to him from far away. "I have loved you with an everlasting love; therefore I have continued my faithfulness to you."

Jeremiah 31:3 ESV

"Eye has not seen, nor ear heard, nor have entered into the heart of man the things which God has prepared for those who love Him."

1 Corinthians 2:9 NKJV

I love those who love me; those who look for me find me.

Proverbs 8:17 The Message

"A new command I give you: Love one another. As I have loved you, so you must love one another. By this all men will know that you are my disciples, if you love one another."

John 13:34-35

I, the Lord your God, am a jealous God who will not share your affection with any other god! I do not leave unpunished the sins of those who hate me. But I lavish my love on those who love me and obey my commands, even for a thousand generations.

Exodus 20:5-6 NLT

Reflections on Love

Marriage

Give honor to marriage, and remain faithful to one another in marriage. God will surely judge people who are immoral and those who commit adultery.

Hebrews 13:4 NLT

Confess your trespasses to one another, and pray for one another, that you may be healed.

James 5:16 NKJV

Husbands, live with your wives in an understanding way, showing honor to the woman as the weaker vessel, since they are heirs with you of the grace of life, so that your prayers may not be hindered.

1 Peter 3:7 ESV

"'For this reason a man will leave his father and mother and be united to his wife, and the two will become one flesh.' So they are no longer two, but one. Therefore what God has joined together, let man not separate."

Mark 10:7-9

Marry and have sons and daughters; find wives for your sons and give your daughters in marriage

Jeremiah 29:6

Wives, submit to your husbands as to the Lord. For the husband is the head of the wife as Christ is the head of the church, his body, of which he is the Savior. Now as the church submits to Christ, so also wives should submit to their husbands in everything.

Ephesians 5:22-24

Let the husband render to his wife the affection due her, and likewise also the wife to her husband.

1 Corinthians 7:3 NKJV

A hearty wife invigorates her husband, but a frigid woman is cancer in the bones.

Proverbs 12:4 THE MESSAGE

To the married I give this charge (not I, but the Lord): the wife should not separate from her husband.

1 Corinthians 7:10 ESV

He who finds a wife finds a good thing, and obtains favor from the LORD.

Proverbs 18:22 NKJV

Parents can provide their sons with an inheritance of houses and wealth, but only the LORD can give an understanding wife.

Proverbs 19:14 NLT

Charm is deceitful, and beauty is vain, but a woman who fears the LORD is to be praised.

Proverbs 31:30 ESV

Reflections on Marriage

Patience

But those who wait on the LORD shall renew their strength; they shall mount up with wings like eagles, they shall run and not be weary, they shall walk and not faint.

Isaiah 40:31 NKJV

The LORD is good to those who wait for him, to the soul who seeks him.

Lamentations 3:25 ESV

I waited patiently for the LORD to help me, and he turned to me and heard my cry.

Psalm 40:1 NLT

You also be patient. Establish your hearts, for the coming of the Lord is at hand.

James 5:8 NKJV

The Lord is not slow in keeping his promise, as some understand slowness. He is patient with you, not wanting anyone to perish, but everyone to come to repentance.

2 Peter 3:9

Learn to be patient, so that you will please God and be given what he has promised.

Hebrews 10:36 CEV

Better is the end of a thing than its beginning, and the patient in spirit is better than the proud in spirit.

Ecclesiastes 7:8 ESV

Rest in the LORD, and wait patiently for Him; do not fret because of him who prospers in his way, because of the man who brings wicked schemes to pass.

Psalm 37:7 NKJV

Wait for the LORD; be strong and take heart and wait for the LORD.

Psalm 27:14

Consider it pure joy, my brothers, whenever you face trials of many kinds, because you know that the testing of your faith develops perseverance. Perseverance must finish its work so that you may be mature and complete, not lacking anything.

James 1:2-4

That is why God had mercy on me, so that Christ Jesus could use me as a prime example of his great patience with even the worst sinners. Then others will realize that they, too, can believe in him and receive eternal life.

1 Timothy 1:16 NLT

Whoever is slow to anger is better than the mighty, and he who rules his spirit than he who takes a city.

Proverbs 16:32 ESV

Reflections on Patience

Perseverance

Blessed is the man who endures temptation; for when he has been approved, he will receive the crown of life which the Lord has promised to those who love Him.

James 1:12 NKJV

"Everyone will hate you because of your allegiance to me. But those who endure to the end will be saved."

Matthew 10:22 NLT

You need to persevere so that when you have done the will of God, you will receive what he has promised.

Hebrews 10:36

Therefore, be steadfast, immovable, always abounding in the work of the Lord, knowing that in the Lord your labor is not in vain.

1 Corinthians 15:58 ESV

We also rejoice in our sufferings, because we know that suffering produces perseverance; perseverance, character; and character, hope. And hope does not disappoint us, because God has poured out his love into our hearts by the Holy Spirit, whom he has given us.

Romans 5:3-5

"The one who endures to the end will be saved."

Matthew 24:13 ESV

"Because you have obeyed my command to persevere, I will protect you from the great time of testing that will come upon the whole world to test those who belong to this world."

Revelation 3:10 NLT

"Be strong and do not let your hands be weak, for your work shall be rewarded!"

2 Chronicles 15:7 NKJV

Let us throw off everything that hinders and the sin that so easily entangles, and let us run with perseverance the race marked out for us.

Hebrews 12:1

Let us not grow weary while doing good, for in due season we shall reap if we do not lose heart.

Galatians 6:9 NKJV

All who win the victory will be given these blessings. I will be their God, and they will be my people.

Revelation 21:7 CEV

For we share in Christ, if indeed we hold our original confidence firm to the end.

Hebrews 3:14 ESV

Reflections on Perseverance

Prayer

"When you pray, go into your room, close the door and pray to your Father, who is unseen. Then your Father, who sees what is done in secret, will reward you."

Matthew 6:6

"It shall come to pass that before they call, I will answer; and while they are still speaking, I will hear."

Isaiah 65:24 NKJV

"Whatever you ask in prayer, you will receive, if you have faith."

Matthew 21:22 ESV

The earnest prayer of a righteous person has great power and wonderful results.

James 5:16 NLT

Be anxious for nothing, but in everything by prayer and supplication, with thanksgiving, let your requests be made known to God; and the peace of God, which surpasses all understanding, will guard your hearts and minds through Christ Jesus.

Philippians 4:6-7 NKJV

For the eyes of the Lord are on the righteous and his ears are attentive to their prayer.

1 Peter 3:12

"Truly, truly, I say to you, whatever you ask of the Father in my name, he will give it to you. Until now you have asked nothing in my name. Ask, and you will receive, that your joy may be full."

John 16:23-24 ESV

"I say to you, whatever things you ask when you pray, believe that you receive them, and you will have them."

Mark 11:24 NKJV

While Jesus was here on earth, he offered prayers and pleadings, with a loud cry and tears, to the one who could deliver him out of death. And God heard his prayers because of his reverence for God.

Hebrews 5:7 NLT

"Call upon me in the day of trouble; I will deliver you, and you will honor me."

Psalm 50:15

The LORD is near to all who call on him, to all who call on him in truth. He fulfills the desires of those who fear him; he hears their cry and saves them.

Psalm 145:18-19

"In those days when you pray, I will listen. If you look for me in earnest, you will find me when you seek me."

Jeremiah 29:12-13 NLT

Reflections on Prayer

Rest

"Come to me, all you who are weary and burdened, and I will give you rest. Take my yoke upon you and learn from me, for I am gentle and humble in heart, and you will find rest for your souls."

Matthew 11:28-29

"In returning and rest you shall be saved; in quietness and in trust shall be your strength."

Isaiah 30:15 ESV

My soul finds rest in God alone; my salvation comes from him. He alone is my rock and my salvation; he is my fortress, I will never be shaken.

Psalm 62:1-2

"My Presence will go with you, and I will give you rest."

Exodus 33:14 NKJV

The LORD your God in your midst, the Mighty One, will save; He will rejoice over you with gladness, He will quiet you with His love, He will rejoice over you with singing.

Zephaniah 3:17 NKJV

My people will live in safety, quietly at home. They will be at rest.

Isaiah 32:18 NLT

You let me rest in fields of green grass. You lead me to streams of peaceful water, and you refresh my life. You are true to your name, and you lead me along the right paths.

Psalm 23:2-3 CEV

I will lie down and sleep in peace, for you alone, O LORD, make me dwell in safety.

Psalm 4:8

He who dwells in the shelter of the Most High will rest in the shadow of the Almighty. I will say of the LORD, "He is my refuge and my fortress, my God, in whom I trust."

Psalm 91:1-2

"Stand in the ways and see, and ask for the old paths, where the good way is, and walk in it; then you will find rest for your souls."

Jeremiah 6:16 NKJV

The fear of the LORD leads to life, and whoever has it rests satisfied; he will not be visited by harm.

Proverbs 19:23 ESV

The LORD himself will fight for you. You won't have to lift a finger in your defense!

Exodus 14:14 NLT

Reflections on Rest

Success

"I know the plans I have for you," declares the LORD, "plans to prosper you and not to harm you, plans to give you hope and a future."

Jeremiah 29:11

For the sake of Christ, then, I am content with weaknesses, insults, hardships, persecutions, and calamities. For when I am weak, then I am strong.

2 Corinthians 12:10 ESV

This Book of the Law shall not depart from your mouth, but you shall meditate in it day and night, that you may observe to do according to all that is written in it. For then you will make your way prosperous, and then you will have good success.

Joshua 1:8 NKJV

It is not that we think we can do anything of lasting value by ourselves. Our only power and success come from God.

2 Corinthians 3:5 NLT

The reward for humility and fear of the LORD is riches and honor and life.

Proverbs 22:4 ESV

The LORD will open to you His good treasure, the heavens, to give the rain to your land in its season, and to bless all the work of your hand. You shall lend to many nations, but you shall not borrow. And the LORD will make you the head and not the tail; you shall be above only, and not be beneath, if you heed the commandments of the LORD your God, which I command you today, and are careful to observe them.

Deuteronomy 28:12-13 NKJV

With me are riches and honor, enduring wealth and prosperity. My fruit is better than fine gold; what I yield surpasses choice silver.

Proverbs 8:18-19

You will enjoy the fruit of your labor. How happy you will be! How rich your life!

Psalm 128:2 NLT

In everything he did he had great success, because the LORD was with him.

1 Samuel 18:14

Remember me, O LORD, when you show favor to your people, come to my aid when you save them, that I may enjoy the prosperity of your chosen ones, that I may share in the joy of your nation and join your inheritance in giving praise.

Psalm 106:4-5

In the morning sow your seed, and in the evening do not withhold your hand; for you do not know which will prosper.

Ecclesiastes 11:6 NKJV

Believe in the LORD your God, and you will be able to stand firm. Believe in his prophets, and you will succeed.

2 Chronicles 20:20 NLT

Reflections on Success

Trust

Trust in the LORD with all your heart, and lean not on your own understanding; in all your ways acknowledge Him, and He shall direct your paths.

Proverbs 3:5-6 NKJV

Those who know your name will trust in you, for you, LORD, have never forsaken those who seek you.

Psalm 9:10

Trust in the LORD, and do good; dwell in the land and befriend faithfulness. Delight yourself in the LORD, and he will give you the desires of your heart.

Psalm 37:3-4 ESV

The LORD is good. When trouble comes, he is a strong refuge. And he knows everyone who trusts in him.

Nahum 1:7 NLT

Surely this is our God; we trusted in him, and he saved us. This is the LORD, we trusted in him; let us rejoice and be glad in his salvation.

Isaiah 25:9

Blessed are all those who put their trust in Him.

Psalm 2:12 NKJV

May the God of hope fill you with all joy and peace as you trust in him, so that you may overflow with hope by the power of the Holy Spirit.

Romans 15:13

Trust in Him at all times, you people; pour out your heart before Him; God is a refuge for us.

Psalm 62:8 NKJV

Behold, God is my salvation; I will trust, and will not be afraid; for the LORD GOD is my strength and my song, and he has become my salvation.

Isaiah 12:2 ESV

"See, I lay a stone in Zion, a chosen and precious cornerstone, and the one who trusts in him will never be put to shame."

1 Peter 2:6

For to this end we both labor and suffer reproach, because we trust in the living God, who is the Savior of all men, especially of those who believe.

1 Timothy 4:10 NKJV

I trust in God, so why should I be afraid? What can mere mortals do to me?

Psalm 56:11 NLT

Reflections on Trust

Wisdom

In him we have redemption through his blood, the forgiveness of sins, in accordance with the riches of God's grace that he lavished on us with all wisdom and understanding.

Ephesians 1:7-8

If you need wisdom – if you want to know what God wants you to do – ask him, and he will gladly tell you. He will not resent your asking.

James 1:5 NLT

Wisdom and knowledge will be the stability of your times, and the strength of salvation; the fear of the LORD is His treasure.

Isaiah 33:6 NKJV

To the man who pleases him, God gives wisdom, knowledge and happiness.

Ecclesiastes 2:26

A wise man is full of strength, and a man of knowledge enhances his might, for by wise guidance you can wage your war, and in abundance of counselors there is victory.

Proverbs 24:5-6 ESV

The fear of the LORD is the beginning of wisdom; a good understanding have all those who do His commandments. His praise endures forever.

Psalm 111:10 NKJV

Wisdom is sweet to your soul. If you find it, you will have a bright future, and your hopes will not be cut short.

Proverbs 24:14 NLT

Wisdom strengthens the wise more than ten rulers of the city.

Ecclesiastes 7:19 NKJV

Happy is the person who finds wisdom and gains understanding. For the profit of wisdom is better than silver, and her wages are better than gold.

Proverbs 3:13-14 NLT

The wisdom from above is first pure, then peaceable, gentle, open to reason, full of mercy and good fruits, impartial and sincere. And a harvest of righteousness is sown in peace by those who make peace.

James 3:17-18 ESV

The fruit of the righteous is a tree of life, and he who wins souls is wise.

Proverbs 11:30

Oh, the depth of the riches of the wisdom and knowledge of God! How unsearchable his judgments, and his paths beyond tracing out!

Romans 11:33

Reflections on Wisdom

Worry

Do not be anxious about anything, but in everything, by prayer and petition, with thanksgiving, present your requests to God. And the peace of God, which transcends all understanding, will guard your hearts and your minds in Christ Jesus.

Philippians 4:6-7

When doubts filled my mind, your comfort gave me renewed hope and cheer.

Psalm 94:19 NLT

It is the LORD who goes before you. He will be with you; he will not leave you or forsake you. Do not fear or be dismayed.

Deuteronomy 31:8 ESV

Cast all your anxiety on him because he cares for you.

1 Peter 5:7

"Seek first the kingdom of God and His righteousness, and all these things shall be added to you. Therefore do not worry about tomorrow, for tomorrow will worry about its own things. Sufficient for the day is its own trouble."

Matthew 6:33-34 NKJV

God is greater than our worried hearts and knows more about us than we do ourselves.

1 John 3:20 THE MESSAGE

Cast your burden on the LORD, and He shall sustain you; He shall never permit the righteous to be moved.

Psalm 55:22 NKJV

Worry weighs a person down; an encouraging word cheers a person up.

Proverbs 12:25 NLT

Though I walk in the midst of trouble, you preserve my life; you stretch out your hand against the wrath of my enemies, and your right hand delivers me.

Psalm 138:7 ESV

For God did not give us a spirit of timidity, but a spirit of power, of love and of self-discipline.

2 Timothy 1:7

"For the mountains shall depart and the hills be removed, but My kindness shall not depart from you, nor shall My covenant of peace be removed," says the LORD, who has mercy on you.

Isaiah 54:10 NKJV

The Lord is my helper, so I will not be afraid. What can mere mortals do to me?

Hebrews 13:6 NLT

Reflections on Worry

Worship

Here's what I want you to do, God helping you: Take your everyday, ordinary life – your sleeping, eating, going-to-work, and walking-around life – and place it before God as an offering. Embracing what God does for you is the best thing you can do for him.

Romans 12:1 The Message

Therefore, since we are receiving a kingdom that cannot be shaken, let us be thankful, and so worship God acceptably with reverence and awe, for our "God is a consuming fire."

Hebrews 12:28-29

"God is spirit, and his worshipers must worship in spirit and in truth."

John 4:24

For great is the LORD, and greatly to be praised, and he is to be held in awe above all gods.

1 Chronicles 16:25 ESV

Praise be to the God and Father of our Lord Jesus Christ, who has blessed us in the heavenly realms with every spiritual blessing in Christ. For he chose us in him before the creation of the world to be holy and blameless in his sight.

Ephesians 1:3-4

I praise you because I am fearfully and wonderfully made; your works are wonderful, I know that full well.

Psalm 139:14

Blessed be the God and Father of our Lord Jesus Christ, who according to His abundant mercy has begotten us again to a living hope through the resurrection of Jesus Christ from the dead.

1 Peter 1:3 NKJV

You must worship no other gods, but only the LORD, for he is a God who is passionate about his relationship with you.

Exodus 34:14 NLT

I will thank you forever, because you have done it. I will wait for your name, for it is good, in the presence of the godly.

Psalm 52:9 ESV

Give honor to the LORD for the glory of his name. Worship the LORD in the splendor of his holiness.

Psalm 29:2 NLT

The LORD lives! Praise be to my Rock! Exalted be God, the Rock, my Savior! He is the God who avenges me.

2 Samuel 22:47-48

Reflections on Worship

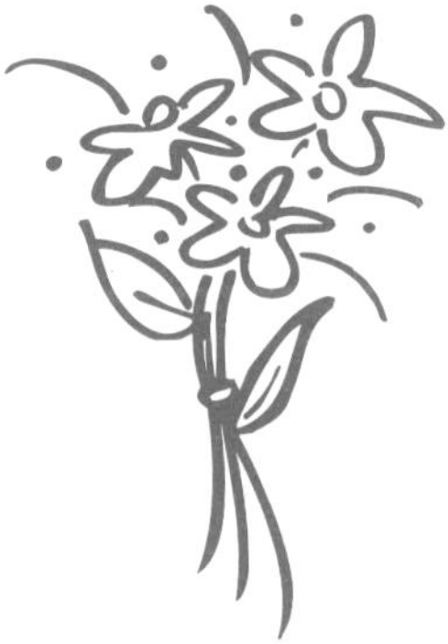